THE ENCOUNTER

VOLUME 1

KI'YANA WINFIELD

The Encounter: Follow Me as I Follow Christ

Copyright © 2025 by Ki'Yana Winfield.

All rights reserved: This book is protected by the copyright laws of the United States of America. No part of this book may be reproduced in any form or by any means, electronic or mechanical, including photocopying, recording, informational storage or retrieval systems, without written permission by the author, except where permitted by law, for the purpose of review, or where otherwise noted.

Unless otherwise noted, Scripture is taken from THE HOLY BIBLE, NEW INTERNATIONAL VERSION ®. Copyright© 1973, 1978, 1984, 201 1 by Biblica, Inc.™. Used by permission of Zondervan.

Scriptures marked KJV are taken from the KING JAMES VERSION (KJV): KING JAMES VERSION, public domain.

Book Layout and Typesetting
DHBonner Vitual Solutions, LLC
www.dhbonner.net

ISBN for Paperback: 9798276713984

Printed in the United States of America

For your encounter with Him

Contents

Disclaimer	vii
The Intro	xiii
Chapter 1	1
The Encounter That Opened My Eyes	
Chapter 2	7
What it Means to Truly Walk with God	
Chapter 3 ¼	17
The Appointment that Changed My Life Forever	
Chapter 3 ½	21
The Encounter: Between Life and Eternity	
Chapter 3 ¾	31
The Revelation: What God Showed Me About Life and Love	
Chapter 4	37
Final Words: The Invitation	
Sneak Peek	45
Afterword	55

Disclaimer

ALL TRUTHS. NO GIMMICKS.

My "Yes"

Hey y'all… I know what you're thinking. "Oh, she's been a die-hard Christian girl her whole life. What could we have in common?" And yeah, you're right, I have. But let me tell you something… this girl has flaws. Plenty. Like, *plenty*. See, I've known Jesus all my life—thank God for my grandmother. She made sure I met Him early. My first encounter with God? I was four years old, on the east side of Detroit, right in our living room, across from the kitchen, on Eastlawn Street, and boy, was I terrified. But we'll save that story for later.

Fast-forward to 2025, and I'm a wife, fourteen years strong, and a mother of five beautiful babies: four girls and one son. And when I say I prayed for that boy, I *prayed*. I mean ugly tears, late nights, "Lord, You said You'd do it" type prayers. And guess what? He did. Because *"All the promises of God are yes and amen."*

DISCLAIMER

(2 Corinthians 1:20). Just wait until I tell you how the enemy tried to trick me into killing my son. He wanted me to destroy the very promise God had just gifted to me. Oh, that sneaky monster.

Now, my husband and me? Whew. Our story's a whole testimony by itself. I've known that man since we were seven. We still laugh about that little Batman tent his mama bought for Christmas one year. And yeah, that's where we had our first kiss. Lord, I was terrified because I just *knew* my butt was grass when I got home if my momma found out. But I didn't know then that the boy in that tent would one day be my husband, my answered prayer.

Growing up, I would go back and forth between Detroit and Lansing — mama in one city, grandparents in another. But every night, I prayed for that boy. Didn't know why. Didn't have a reason; I just felt that I should. Guess my spirit knew something my mind hadn't caught up to yet. By twelve, we were best friends. By eighteen, we were married. By nineteen, parents. By twenty-five? Almost divorced—three times. But "What God has joined together, let no man separate" (Mark 10:9). Not even me! Well, at least the last two times, the first time was all on that man. We're proof that love can fall, but grace can lift it back up again. So stay tuned, because that whole story is coming soon in *"The Purposed Marriage"* and trust me, it's one you'll want to hear all about.

Let me talk about my walk, though, concerning my YES! Yes, I got baptized twice. Once at thirteen but rededicated at thirty-

DISCLAIMER

one. Because, baby, after all the foolery I was in, I knew better. And when you know better, you do better.

> "Anyone, then, who knows the right
> thing to do and fails to do it, commits sin."
> **-James 4:17**

In 2022, I surrendered for real. No more drinking. No more cursing. No more parties. No more halfway Christian. I gave my *whole* life to Christ. Was it hard? A little. But once I made up my mind, baby, it was done! Was it worth it? Absolutely.

Since then, I've opened three businesses, closing two because they were no longer purpose-aligned and one—my salon, *Kii Beauty Bar House of Prayer*—because its season was over. I'd put everything I had into that dream, every dime, every drop of faith, and God said, "Shut it down." I didn't understand it then, but obedience always births overflow.

> "Trust in the Lord with all your heart,
> and lean not on your own understanding."
> **-Proverbs 3:5-6**

And out of that obedience, He birthed *Community Development to Success*, a Kingdom business that builds kingdom outcomes, shifts lives, and impacts nations — one soul and one encounter at a time. In our first year, 2024, we generated $1 million in revenue. *"Now unto Him who is able to do exceedingly, abundantly above all that we ask or think…"* (Ephesians 3:20). You can't tell me my God ain't good!

DISCLAIMER

Also, stay on the lookout for Random Ki Thoughts. When I've got questions, I've *got* questions—and I expect God to answer. And guess what? My God, does He! Every single time, right on time. Sometimes so right on time that I get a little afraid even to ask, because I don't know what He's going to say or if I'll even like His response. But once He speaks, I have to obey.

See, I've learned it's easier not to know and do something than to know and do it, because those consequences are heavy. And according to 2 Peter 2:21, "It would have been better for them not to have known the way of righteousness, than to have known it and then to turn their backs on the sacred command that was passed on to them." Then coming around the corner, Big James with James 4:17: "Therefore to him that knoweth to do good, and doeth it not, to him it is sin" (KJV).

Yeah, I just take the man at His literal word and thug it out! Can you tell I was raised by a praying, God-fearing woman? Because I was (lol).

So yeah, this is a snippet of my story and how I became a woman of God (follower of Jesus Christ), a wife, a mother, and soon to be a multi-millionaire. Not by luck, but by obedience. By alignment. By saying *yes* to the call of God. And that, yes? That "yes" changed everything. Let's go, 'cause this… this is about to be *good*.

*"Follow my example, as
I follow the example of Christ."*
-1 Corinthians 11:1

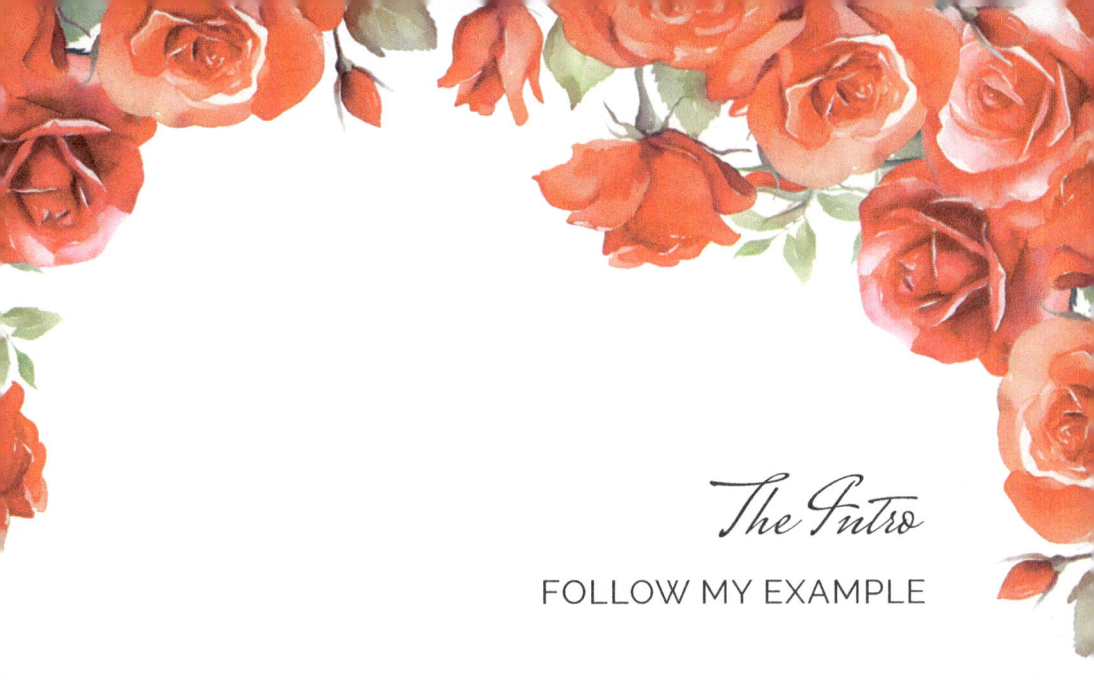

The Intro
FOLLOW MY EXAMPLE

Hey y'all, it's your girl Ki'Yana or Mrs. K, whatever you're comfortable with saying: Believer, Wife, Mom, and Serial Entrepreneur. But before we even start, let me just say… some of y'all were a little too invested in my business. A little nosey, huh? *It's okay*, because now that you're here, you might as well get comfortable. See, I believe everything happens for a reason. If you're holding this book or listening to my voice right now, that means there's something here meant for you.

Now, you know a little bit about me, but I don't know a thing about you. So, before we go any further, make sure you connect with ya girl by joining **The Invested Encounters** community. This is where we can talk, grow, and walk this thing out together between releases because baby, your girl needs rest too. We all do. You can't pour from an empty cup. Email **encounter@communitydts.com** to receive your access code and step-by-step guide to joining.

THE INTRO

Alright, let's get to the reason you picked up this book in the first place. You're probably wondering, *what's all this hype about following God?* And when I say God, I mean Jesus Christ, just so we're clear. What's it really like to walk closely with Him, and why does it matter?

Let me be honest, when I first gave my life to Christ, those were my same questions. I was like, "Okay, Lord… now what? What does this mean? What does it even look like to walk with you every day?" Because the deeper I sought Him, the more I realized I didn't really know Him at all. And if I'm being real, I didn't know *myself* either.

Yeah, I grew up hearing about God. My grandmother prayed over us, told us stories, and made sure we went to church. But the God I *thought* I knew, the One I'd heard about from other people, He was nothing like the One I came to know personally. He was even better! And that's what this set of books, this whole journey, is about. It's about what it truly means to walk in intimacy with God—not religion, not routine, but *relationship.*

So, buckle up, because your girl's about to take you for a ride. And I mean a real one.

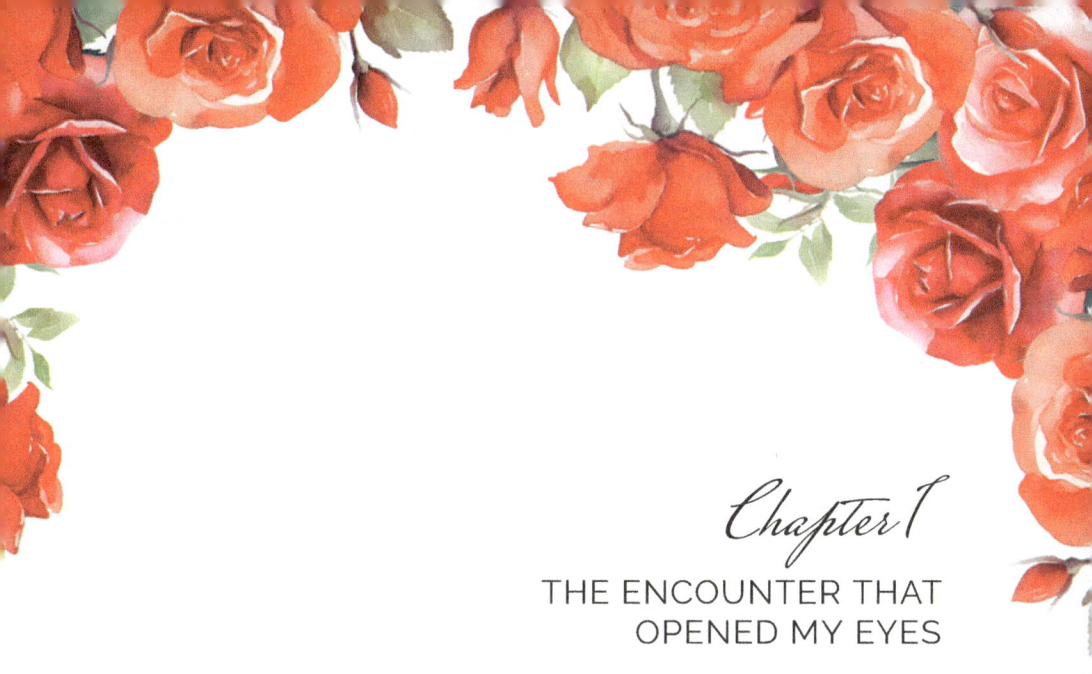

Chapter 1
THE ENCOUNTER THAT OPENED MY EYES

Let's jump right into it. I want to tell you about the second time I personally encountered God. The first time, I was about four, so I'll save that for "The Story Before the Encounters." But this time, I was about sixteen or seventeen, still in high school. Yeah, I used to go out to clubs and drink a little. I know, a bit young for all that, but I was "responsible," or at least that's what I told myself. Doesn't make it right, but that's just where I was at the time.

Now, I always *knew* about God. My grandmother talked about Him and prayed to Him every single day... all day, every day. But I didn't *know* Him for myself. I didn't understand what it meant to actually have a relationship with Him. Just wait until I tell you about the time my grandmother was diagnosed with Stage 3 colon cancer. And let me be real with you, it all came down to my idolizing her.

Baby, I ran to her about *everything*. I felt like I didn't even need God, because she was His best friend. If I needed anything done, she was the plug straight to Him, and that was that. But then God decided to test her faith right in the middle of it all. And let me tell you, it got real, and it got real *fast*. But back to the story...

So, on this one particular day, I had no idea that I was about to meet God for myself, like, for real, for real. It was a Sunday night. There was this pop-up conference at the clubhouse where we used to live. My mom, my three aunts (one biological and two by marriage at the time), and I decided to go. I didn't know what to expect, but I've always loved hearing stories about God and seeing how He moved in people's lives.

It's not that I didn't believe in Him; deep down, I *knew* He was real, I just didn't understand Him yet. Kind of like how you're reading this story right now, you don't actually *know* me, but you have an idea of who I am. You believe what I'm saying because I haven't given you a reason not to. That's how my faith was at that point, I believed, but I didn't *know*.

At this conference, a man from Africa was there to minister. I can't even remember what part he was from, but let me tell you, the authority in his voice was something I'd never experienced before. The way he spoke, you could just feel that whatever power he carried was real. It was authentic. God was *with* that man, no question about it. I also realized God had placed specific people in that room that night to witness what was about to happen, people I knew from school, the neighborhood, and even some family members.

When the man of God began to preach, his message was all about building a *real* relationship with God, not faking it, but being genuine. Every word he spoke went straight to my heart. I remember looking around the room, seeing everyone so locked in, so hungry for more of what he was saying. I can't even recall every word he preached, but the main point was clear: *Get yourself together.* God isn't playing, but He's waiting for you with open arms. Hell is real, but so is His love.

At that point, I knew right from wrong, but still didn't understand God on an intimate level. I wanted to. I wanted to know Him like a best friend, someone who truly had my back. Growing up, I often felt misunderstood and alone, so in that moment, I knew God wanted to meet me that night. I didn't know how, but I could feel it.

Then the preacher gave us instructions: he said everyone could have their own encounter with God if they wanted. The clubhouse was set up like a church, rows of chairs and all. He told everyone to start praying, to call out to God. At first, I was confused. But then people started praying in tongues, and things began *happening*. The preacher walked through the aisles, yielding correction as he was speaking into people's lives, not harshly but with love. And people *knew* God was speaking to them through him.

When he came to our row, my mom and two of my aunts (by marriage) were praying in tongues, and he said their tongues were false. I didn't actually know who he was talking to; all I know is that right then and right there, the Holy Spirit changed them, and they fell out crying. My other aunt and I weren't speaking in tongues, yet she kept saying, "Jesus, Jesus, Jesus," because, baby, one thing we did know was we don't play with demons, and I sat there watching everything, fascinated.

Then the man looked right at me… and walked away. My heart started racing. My mind flooded with every painful memory, every bad thing I'd done, every emotion I'd ever tried to bury. Being the oldest of four, I'd had to grow up fast. My mom is amazing, don't get me wrong, she did what she could to make sure we had a good life. She made mistakes, but she always tried to keep us away from the streets, even though she was caught up in them herself for a while. That's why I lived with my grandparents, and thank God I did, because my grandmother's prayers shaped me into who I am today.

Anyway, back to that night, my heart was pounding, and I told my aunt I had to use the bathroom (which was a lie). I just needed to get out of that room because I couldn't breathe. It felt like I was having a panic attack, like my insides were shaking.

THE ENCOUNTER

When I made it to the bathroom, I closed the door and leaned against the wall, trying to catch my breath. I could still hear the preacher's voice echoing through the walls. And right there, I broke down. *"Okay, God, you win. I'm tired. I can't do this by myself anymore. I can't do this by myself anymore. I just can't."* Then everything went black.

Next thing I knew, someone was grabbing me, people were surrounding me, and then darkness again (they said I tore them folks' bathroom up). I got a quick glimpse of myself, rolling on the floor and screaming like a mad woman. Then I heard a firm, calm voice say, *"Loose her now and come out of her."* In that instant, my mind went quiet. My body went still. My soul felt *free*.

When I opened my eyes, everything looked different. The room was brighter, like ten times brighter, and people were staring at me with their mouths open. I was confused, like, *What's going on? Why's everyone looking at me like that?* Then I realized I was on the floor, hair messed up, shoes twisted… and I had no idea how I got there. The preacher asked how I felt. I just started crying and thanking him. He helped me up and said, *"That was God, my dear, not me."* And that's when it hit me: God had just revealed Himself to me, for real. Inside, I felt completely new, like I'd been reborn. I could see, feel, and sense things differently. The world felt heavy and dirty, but I felt *clean*. I knew there were things I could no longer do or even be around.

As we were leaving, one of my classmates stopped me, worried. "Hey, are you okay?" he asked. I smiled and said, "Nah, I'm better than okay." However, afterward, I began to sense people's emotions and intentions. It was overwhelming. I was terrified of sinning, even lying, because I didn't want to lose that peace I'd just experienced. So I didn't tell anyone what really happened, not even my mom. I was scared they wouldn't understand.

Eventually, I asked my mom to take me to my grandmother's house because I knew she'd know what to do. I stayed there for a whole week, barely leaving my room. I was scared of the world; it just felt wrong to me. My grandmother prayed with me, taught me what had happened, and that I'd gone through *deliverance*. She explained how to stay free. I'll never forget what she told me:

> When a house is swept clean, the demon comes back to check on it. And if it finds an open door, it'll return with seven more, stronger than itself. So stay prayed up. Keep your heart clean. Never teach your heart to lie.

Those words stuck with me. When I went back home and returned to school, I was different. I didn't party. I didn't curse. I barely hung out with friends because certain things just made me uncomfortable. But eventually, I let my guard down and, like they say, give the enemy a crack, and he'll make a hole. And that's exactly what happened. But that's a story for another time.

Chapter 2
WHAT IT MEANS TO TRULY WALK WITH GOD

So AGAIN, picture this: me, twenty years old, just doing life. I knew *about* God because my grandmother prayed all the time from sunrise to sunset; that woman stayed on her knees. But knowing *about* Him and *knowing* Him? That's two different things.

I didn't have a real relationship. I wasn't against God. I believed He was real, no doubt, but He just felt far away. I was living life the way I thought best, making my own decisions, trying to fill the empty spaces with people and things that didn't actually heal me. And then boom, this happens. I just had a newborn, she isn't even a week old yet, and I got a call from my grandma. She tells me she's been diagnosed with stage 3 colon cancer.

My whole family was terrified because my grandma is our backbone. She's our strength, our foundation. And in that moment, I felt like everything was about to collapse. But something rose up in me, and I said, *"There's no way God would let His servant go out like this. That don't even make sense."*

Grandma called all her kids, and we were thinking the same thing: she's been through a lot, she lived a life full of battles and victories, but this? This didn't seem like the way her story should end. She did all the appointments, the tests, the surgery to examine the cancer, and then the doctor walked in and said the words we feared: stage 3 colon cancer. We tried to prepare ourselves for whatever God would allow, but deep down, our spirits kept saying, *"She's going to be healed."*

Then she remembered what God had said to her and shared with us what Aunt V had said God had spoken to her. God had told her to tell my grandma, "You're going to go through a trauma, but I'm going to bring you out."

And then my granny told us about another time when she was at church, and this man was praying for her. In the middle of the prayer, God told him to tell her, "Don't worry. You're going to live a long life… a long, long, long life," and he kept repeating it over and over. When she said that, something hit me. *This is the moment He was talking about. This right here.*

"Ma, your faith is on trial right now," I told her. "You just gotta believe." She just said, "Sweetheart, you never know what something really feels like until you're in that very seat." We kept telling her, "Grandma, the way you believe in God, we believe too. You don't have to take chemo. Just trust Him." And even though I didn't yet fully know God for myself, I trusted what He told her. I trusted her faith.

My grandma had a relationship with God unlike anything I'd ever seen. Even after her son was murdered, she became even stronger, as if something in her shifted, like she knew something we didn't. Her posture changed, since she now knew what it meant to truly rest in God—knowing Him as her refuge, provider, and friend… for real, for real. Anything she prayed for, anything she needed, He provided almost instantly. Like Amazon Prime, I'm talking same-day, doorstep delivery, sometimes the same hour. So, I couldn't imagine her having cancer and God not healing her.

I told her, "Grandma, get your faith up. Pray, do something. Ask God what's going on." And that's when God started talking to her… but what I didn't realize is that He was also coming after *me*.

> "God chastens the one he loves"
> **--Hebrews 12:6 NIV**

At the time, I was two years into my marriage and going through a rough season, not as bad as I thought, but enough to shake me. Looking back, I realize I had put my grandma in a place only God should've been. I relied on her for everything, because who would I be without her? Nevertheless, God was calling me to depend on Him—to know Him for myself.

Anyway, Grandma eventually decided to try chemo. Scared? I was terrified! Because who wouldn't be when death is possibly knocking at the frame of your heart? I was terrified of losing my momma, my best friend, my everything, especially when they explained all the scary side effects: falling out hair, skin darkening, weakness, throwing up. I was like, *"Girl, absolutely not. "Nah, this don't even sound right."*

Yet she decided to go through with it, and if you know my granny, what she says goes—no ifs, ands, or buts about it, so there we have it. They put the chemo port in her chest... and every time she went in, for treatment, the port flipped—literally flipped inside her body so they couldn't access it. It happened again and again.

One night, she called me into her room and asked me to help fix it. And I told her, "Grandma, maybe it's flipping for a reason. Maybe God is showing you that you don't need this... that you're healed and to stop putting that poison in your body." No shade to those who take it, I just knew what God said, she didn't need it, and I stand on that! Because the wild thing was that chemo wasn't affecting her the way it affects other people. Her hair grew longer. Her nails grew stronger. Her skin looked beautiful. The only thing different was that the tips of her thumbs turned a little purple. That was it. I told her, "You don't see the signs? God is with you."

Fast forward, and she had to drink a solution before they rechecked her for cancer. That day, it was storming like crazy, thunder shaking the house, lightning lighting up the whole sky. I knew in my spirit she was praying. My grandfather told everyone to go home and rest, but I couldn't. As soon as everyone fell asleep, I snuck out and drove to the hospital. The hallways were dark and empty, creepy, honestly, but I pushed through because I knew I needed to be with her.

When I walked into her room, she started laughing, like, "Girl, you heard all that outside?" We talked, laughed, then she said, "Come sit down so we can pray. And I want *you* to pray." I had never really prayed out loud before. But something came over me, and I prayed from a place I didn't even know I had. When I finished, she looked at me and said, "You know the very thing you place before God, He'll take it away. He's a jealous God."

And instantly, I knew God was speaking to me. I had placed her before Him. My heart dropped. When I went home, I prayed again, really prayed, and apologized. I felt something shift. I knew something was about to happen.

Not long after, Grandma came home, then went back for her results. Her doctor was never a religious man. Every time she told him, "Praise the Lord," he just ignored it. But this time, she walked in saying, "Hallelujah," and he said, "Praise the Lord." She slapped his arm like, "What did you say?" And he repeated it: "Praise the Lord." Then he told her the news that changed everything: *"Mrs. Parker, you don't have cancer anymore."* She shouted, "Hallelujah! Praise the Lord! Thank you, Jesus!

From that day forward, I knew I had to step back, not to leave her, but to build my own relationship with God. To understand Him for myself. Yes, it created distance. Yes, it changed our relationship. But it was intentional. It was necessary. And from that day on… I was never the same. In that moment, I felt God's presence like never before. When I came to, YES, he really did it! I was crying, confused, but convinced. And for the first time in my life, I knew without a doubt that God was real, not just in the Bible, not just in my grandma's prayers, but *real* in my life.

Now here's the thing: when God steps into your life, that's not the end, that's the beginning. Because after that day, I had to *learn* how to walk with Him. It wasn't always easy. I had to unlearn habits, distance myself from things and people that didn't feed my spirit, and start spending real time with Him. I spoke to God as I would to a close friend. I'd wake up and say, *"Good morning, God."* I'd vent when I was frustrated, cry when I was confused, and ask Him questions, and somehow, He'd always find a way to answer.

And I mean, He answered fast! Sometimes it was through a verse or a song, and sometimes through a random moment that spoke right to my situation.

Walking in a close relationship with God isn't about being perfect. It's about being *present.* It's showing up even when you don't feel holy enough, even when you've messed up, even when you're not sure He's listening because He *is.*
Here's what I've learned:

1. **Talk to God daily.** Don't wait until church on Sunday. Talk to Him in your car, your shower, your kitchen. He's not limited to a building.

2. **Be honest.** God can't heal what you hide. If you're angry, say it. If you're scared, admit it. He already knows, He's just waiting for you to open the door.

3. **Listen.** Prayer isn't just talking *to* God; it's also listening *for* Him. Sometimes His silence is protection. Sometimes His "not yet" is preparation.

4. **Stay in His Word.** The Bible isn't just a rulebook; it's a love letter. It reveals who God is, and when you know Him, you recognize His voice more quickly.

5. **Guard your space.** Once you invite God in, everything that doesn't align with Him will start to feel off. Pay attention to that. That's His Spirit guiding you.

6. **He is Love.** Over time, I realized that walking closely with God feels a lot like falling in love.

You want to spend time with Him. You think about Him when you wake up and when you go to bed. You start craving His presence the way you used to crave attention from people. And that's why I say He's not just my King, my Father, or my friend. He's also my man, the One who loves me better than anyone ever could.

Because when you learn to love God first, everything else starts to make sense. So, if you're reading this and you've been searching for something or someone to fill that space in your heart… start with Him. He's not waiting for you to be perfect. He's just waiting for you to say, *"Okay, God, you win."* And when you do, everything changes. Just like my life did the moment I thought I was just going to a dentist appointment, but God had other plans. Don't trip. I'm going to tell you all about it!

THE ENCOUNTER

RANDOM KI THOUGHT

Listen, don't judge me when I say this, but I see God as my King, my Father, my Governor, my Best Friend... and yes, my *Man*.

Go ahead, raise your eyebrows. I know you want to. But listen, I promise there's a reason behind that. Think about it: when you're tired of being alone and tired of carrying everything by yourself, your heart starts craving a partnership. You want someone you can talk to, someone who gets you, someone you can do life with. And in your mind, you start building a list: tall, fine, loving, supportive, good with family, knows how to lead, and yeah, knows how to pray. You've got boxes to check, and you start dreaming about what that person might look like, sound like, how they make you feel.

Now imagine putting that same energy into choosing who you'll spend *eternity* with. Because when this life is over, that's it. There's no *"God, I'm sorry. Take me back,"* or *"Let's try again."* There are no second chances once the lights go out on this side. Baby, it's OVER!

So, if you're going to choose someone to build with and to walk into eternity with, you'd better choose wisely. And that's where my second encounter really began. The day I thought I was just going to a dentist appointment, but God had other plans. Plans to meet me in another way that I'd never forget.

Chapter 3 1/4
THE APPOINTMENT THAT CHANGED MY LIFE FOREVER

It was a regular midday morning—nothing special about it. I was scheduled for oral surgery. They needed to expose a canine tooth embedded in the roof of my mouth to align it for my braces. Simple, right? At least that's what I thought. Now, if you know me, you know I don't play about the dentist: needles, drills, those bright lights. No, ma'am. No, sir. So, I asked for medication to help calm my nerves before the procedure.

My regular dental office couldn't perform the procedure, so they referred me to an out-of-network specialist, Dr. J, about an hour outside of town. Since I couldn't drive afterward, my husband, my man, capital M, drove me. We pulled up to this office and y'all… it was beautiful. Bright, clean, modern, with soft music playing that gave off a spa vibe. I remember thinking, *Okay, Lord, this isn't too bad.*

The staff was pleasant and welcoming, smiling like they didn't have a worry in the world. But me? My nerves were on ten thousand. Like the time after I had my fifth baby, and a lady tried to kidnap her right under my nose. Yeah, I know. Just imagine how I felt, but we'll talk more about this in Volume 2, so back to what I was saying. Then I heard my name.

"Kiyana Winfield?"

My heart dropped. I looked at my husband, and he just smiled, stood up, and hugged me. "Bae, you're gonna be okay," he whispered. So, I took a deep breath and followed the assistant to the back, every step feeling like a countdown.

The room was bright and sterile, that sharp white light you can feel in your soul. The doctor and his assistant were kind and professional. They talked me through everything and told me it would only take about thirty minutes. After they put the gas mask on me, I tried to relax, remembering my grandmother once telling me about when she was in labor.

> She said the pain was so intense that she asked for something—*anything*—to help ease it. They gave her laughing gas, and when they placed the mask over her face, she pulled on it hard, hoping it would knock the pain away. But instead of relief, all she really got was the smell of that rubber gas mask.

So I told myself, "You'll be fine, Kiyana. Breathe normal but pull fast and hard. It's just gas." But the moment they turned it on, my spirit whispered *something's not right*. I heard Dr. J say to his assistant, "Turn it up a bit more." At the time, I didn't think much of it. But the second that gas hit, my body got *heavy*. My eyes flew open, and I knew.

Something was off.

I started praying not out loud, but in tongues, in my mind. Then, suddenly, everything around me began to distort. The buzzing of the tools, the movement of their hands, all slowed down like time itself was melting. My heart started racing so fast I could hear it pounding in my head.

Then the sound faded.
    And just like that…
    everything went black.

Chapter 3 1/2
THE ENCOUNTER: BETWEEN LIFE AND ETERNITY

So, when I tell you I felt myself leaving my body, I mean exactly that. This wasn't imagination. This wasn't nerves. Something inside me told me *you're crossing over*. The room began to blur, colors blending together, and sounds stretching out like echoes in a tunnel. I could still see Dr. J and his assistant, their hands moving over me, but they looked… far away.

My body was still there, but I was somewhere else.
   I felt myself *sliding*.
   Not like falling, no. It was smoother…
   Like floating backward through air thick as honey.

And even though I was terrified, a strange peace started to settle over me. Then came the sound. A high-pitched whirring, maybe the dentist's drill, but to me, it felt like the sound of my *soul* screaming, "Something's wrong!"

That's when I realized I was dying.

My mind split in two, one part praying desperately to stay alive, the other… just observing, like I was watching a movie of my own life. And then I saw it. I was standing in a completely black space. No walls. No ground. No light. Just me… floating. Over what seemed to be billions of never-ending stairs!

The air wasn't cold or warm; it was *nothing.*
    And yet, I felt everything.

Images started flashing before my eyes, scenes moving faster than thought. I saw my husband standing at a counter, crying. A nurse walked up to him; He was wearing a white shirt and jeans. I remembered her telling him, "She didn't make it." He dropped his head, tears streaming down his face, barely breathing, grabbed his keys, and drove to my grandmother's house. In the very same truck we were driving then!

Oh, my God! I began to panic; it seemed so real and present! I wanted to reach out, scream, *I'm still here! I'm still here!*
    But I couldn't.

THE ENCOUNTER

The next moment, I was somewhere else... a funeral? My funeral, I believe. I could see it from above. It was an all-black casket with gold handles. It was beautiful, but the burial site was empty. No one was there. No one! I felt this wave of sadness, and then my mind went there like, Am I really that bad? No one showed up to my funeral? No way I'm that mean. Lord, what are you trying to tell me?

Then I noticed two massive beings standing beside me, one on each side. Think of a penny on the ground in between two skyscrapers. Yeah, that's massive! Not men... *angels (Seraphim's to be exact)*. Huge. Radiant. Powerful. Their presence felt like thunder and peace at the same time.
   Beautiful, I tell you, Beautiful!

Well, at least the wings I saw
   (Oh, My Gosh... and SOOO many wings)
   And they spoke.
   Not with mouths, but directly into my spirit.
   One said, *"She's smart."*
   The other laughed, *"Now I see why God chose her."*

And then they both looked at me and said, "It's not time yet. You almost made it. You almost made it."
   Almost.

And in that moment, I understood that I wasn't meant to stay there. Not yet. But I begged. I pleaded. "Please! Let me go back to my family. Let me tell them what I've seen. Let me tell them to be happy." "God... I promise I won't be mean to them anymore. I won't respond out of anger, past hurt, or frustration. I see it now! The things I thought mattered don't mean anything. The material stuff doesn't matter at all." "I know I messed up. I really do. But if you let me go back, I'll walk in love this time. I'll be different. Please, God... I can't end my life like this. This isn't who I am."

Then, I found myself reflecting on the rich man who descended into hell, pleading with Abraham to share his experiences with his brothers so that they would change (Luke 16:19-31). But see, I wanted to go back myself, "Lord send me!" I felt a profound sense of helplessness, realizing that there was no turning back.

Yet, I still begged, "Dear Lord, please let me go back! My husband, Lord, my husband!" "My husband deserves better, and so do my kids. Please, let me go back and love them the right way. I have to make this right. I understand now, Lord. I get it." "I cry out to You because I know You hear me... and I just need another chance to love them like You've loved me."

And the angels just smiled... like parents watching their child finally "get it." Then, out of nowhere, laughter filled the air, not mocking, but joyful, like heaven itself was smiling. A bright white light appeared ahead of me, not blinding, but *alive*. It pulsed with warmth, love, and understanding so deep I can't even describe it. And just when I reached for it.

ZIP!
 I was back.
 Back in the dentist's chair.
 Back in my body.
 The nurse's voice cut through the fog:
 "You're doing great! It's not time yet. Good job."

Then darkness again.

This time, the weightlessness was stronger—like being caught between two worlds, my body still fighting to breathe, my soul just drifting. I felt myself moving again, floating backward this time into what looked like a *line*. A long, endless line.

And listen, y'all might laugh, but I'm just being honest, there were people in that line. All kinds. To be more specific, I was standing in line behind two heterosexual men, and something about the whole scene just felt *off*. Deep down, I knew something wasn't right. They seemed so content, so sure of themselves, just as happy as they wanted to be, like they didn't even realize we were about to meet God. They called themselves a couple, and hey, call me what you want, I'm not judging them but myself, because, honey, what was I doing in the same line as them… I knew something was wrong. I must have seriously messed up to be in the same line as them. *Oh my Lord, I must be in the wrong line! I'm going to hell! Oh No! I'm going to hell!*

STORY TIME

I honestly believed I was headed to hell. For real. Why? Because I had my fair share of straddling that fence, and I knew God didn't play about that same sex stuff. We're talking Sodom and Gomorrah type of serious. Deep down, I thought, *I must've crossed the line one too many times.*

It all started when I was about eight or nine years old. One of my childhood friends, someone I trusted, touched me and exposed me to sexual things with a teddy bear in a way that wasn't right. I knew it was wrong, but I was confused because it felt good. And since it was a girl who first touched me like that, one of my best friends at that time planted a lie in my mind. I started to believe it might be okay because I liked the way it felt. But it wasn't. It was a lie, a wound.

Years later, I found out she had only done that because her older sister had been doing the same thing and had planted that seed in her. My heart broke for her, and I forgave her. But the damage was already done. That moment planted a seed of confusion deep inside me, a seed that followed me for years. I couldn't understand why something that felt good could also feel so wrong. But the truth is, it was seriously wrong.

Eventually, God revealed the truth to me. He showed me that the root of my struggle came from that wrong seed one planted in curiosity, lust, and deceit, but watered by trauma, vulnerability, hurt, and abandonment. I had been trying to cover that pain with temporary pleasures, but nothing ever filled the emptiness inside me.

Real healing didn't start until I surrendered everything to God. That's when He reached into the broken places I had buried for so long and began to show me who I truly was in Him. I realized I'm not what happened to me. I'm not my past mistakes. God delivered me completely and set me free from the spirit that once tried to define me. What the enemy meant for evil, God restored my identity, my peace, and my purpose.

But even after all that, there came this moment, the moment of judgment. And that's when I realized God wasn't finished with me yet. When I caught myself in this long line, murmuring, complaining under my breath, saying, "I can't go to hell. I just can't." "Why is this line taking so long? What's going on?"

And clear as day, I heard a voice—not angry, but firm—say:
"Even now, you're complaining before meeting me."

That shut me right up. Then everything went dark again. The darkness wasn't scary this time. It was deep like the universe itself. And floating in that blackness, I saw small, glowing lights, tiny orbs, like souls scattered across eternity. And somehow, I knew this was the space between life and forever. I was in the center of it. No sound. No feeling. Just peace.

>No fear.
>No pain.
>No sense of time.
>Just stillness,
>Yet I was completely aware and completely free.
>And for the first time ever…
>I wasn't worried about anything.
>Not bills, not responsibilities, not even death.
>I was home.
>At least, that's how it felt.

Then, out of nowhere, I heard my name again.
   "Kiyana… Kiyana…"

It sounded funny, like a chorus of voices, echoing through laughter, calling me back. The assistant's voice came through, faint but real: "Stay away from the white light." But y'all… that light was *beautiful*. It didn't feel dangerous; it felt *safe*. As I drifted toward it, I could feel every weight from this life peeling off of me, every regret, every fear, every anxiety gone. And right before I touched the light, I felt myself *release*.

No resistance.
No pain.
Just pure peace.

I entered the light and thought, *Well, that's it. I'm gone.* And I was okay with that. Because being in that space, it wasn't like anything I'd ever known. There was nobody there. No sound. No thought of "earth." Just *oneness*. It was like I was sitting in the middle of creation itself, the center of the universe, and for the first time, I understood what true peace was. Then, suddenly...

ZIP!
I was back again.

This time, really back. Sitting in that dentist chair, blinking like, *Wait... what?* And y'all, the first thing I thought was, "Why did you bring me back? It was nicer over there!" Ten seconds later, my hearing returned. The dental assistant was talking. I could see her lips moving before the sound caught up. And then... I started laughing. Like, deep, belly laughing, tears flowing because the whole thing felt unreal.

Thirty to forty minutes had passed in that room. But to me? It felt like only three. I started to think, "God, did you really bring me to the dentist's office to die? Really, the dentist! Is this where my life would've ended? Oh, my God!"

That experience changed me forever. Something in me had shifted permanently. And even though it might sound wild to you, I came back knowing things I'd never known before. Not facts, truths. Things my soul understood that my mind had never been able to grasp.

Chapter 3 3/4
THE REVELATION: WHAT GOD SHOWED ME ABOUT LIFE AND LOVE

When I came back, everything looked the same... but nothing *felt* the same. It's wild. The dentist was cleaning his tools, the assistant was smiling as if nothing had happened, and I was sitting there, blinking, trying to act normal while my whole soul was still somewhere between heaven and earth. My body was here, but my spirit? Still catching up.

I remember thinking, *What just happened?* And clear as day, I heard in my heart, *"You just lived what you must preach: LOVE & intimacy with Me."* Instantly, everything slowed down. My thoughts stopped racing. The little things that used to stress me out just... didn't matter. All I could think about was *love*. Not the kind we chase here, the romantic kind, or the conditional kind. But real, raw, all-encompassing, God-breathed love. Because in that space, that still, weightless, endless space, that's all there was. *Just love.*

I started to realize that all the noise we make down here, all the striving, the comparison, the hustling, the "look at me" moments, all fade when you stand in the presence of the One who *is* love. And what He pressed on my spirit right then was simple but heavy: "The meaning of life... is love." At first, I thought that sounded too easy. But the more I sat with it, the more I understood. Love is the only thing that carries over when this life ends.

> Not money.
> Not fame.
> Not business titles or accomplishments.
> Only love — the kind that mirrors God's heart.

THE LESSONS THAT STAYED WITH ME

When I woke up from that encounter, I didn't just come back with peace; I came back with a list of truths etched into my spirit, as if God Himself had taken a pen and written them down, rewiring how I see everything. Let me share them with you. Maybe they'll sit in your heart like they do in mine.

- Some things in life, you simply can't control.

- You can only choose how you respond, how you love, and how you move forward.

- If someone you love doesn't love you back, release them. Yet love them from a place of forgiveness, not for them, but for you.

- Don't mourn what didn't return because love isn't ownership, it's reflection. Let God redirect that love where it's needed most.

- Live fully in the moment.

- Don't rush through your blessings trying to reach the next thing. Each season, even the uncomfortable ones, is part of your training ground.

- Love doesn't mean limitation.

- Love freely, but don't lose yourself trying to keep someone else. God never asked you to shrink to fit inside someone else's story.

- We will all leave this world alone.

- But what waits beyond isn't fear, it's freedom. The pain belongs to those left behind; those who cross over find peace beyond understanding.

- At the end of the day, love is the only thing that matters.

- It's the thread that ties heaven to earth, the one thing that never dies.

When I came home that day, I couldn't stop smiling. My husband thought it was the meds wearing off, but it wasn't that. It was a revelation. For the first time, I understood why God calls us to walk in love. Because everything else, the rules, the rituals, the church titles, all mean nothing if love isn't at the center. Paul said it best:

> "If I speak in the tongues of men and of angels, but have not love, I am nothing."
> **-1 Corinthians 13:1**

That hit different after what I experienced. And let me tell you, I don't fear death anymore. I don't rush through life anymore either. Because when you've stood in that in-between space, and felt peace so thick it silences everything you've ever worried about, you realize how fragile and precious this whole thing is.

You start hugging your people tighter.
You start forgiving faster.
You stop wasting time on petty arguments or fake friendships.
You wake up each day grateful because you *know* what it means to get a second chance. And baby, not everybody does.

So, when I tell you to follow Christ, I'm not saying it from a place of "church talk." I'm saying it from experience—from the other side of consciousness, from that space where nothing but truth survives; whether you meet Him here in faith, or there after this life, you *will* meet Him. And I'd rather meet Him as

His daughter than as a stranger. That's why I keep saying, *get it right the first time.*

Don't play with eternity. You don't want to be the one saying, *"God, give me another chance,"* when the clock has already stopped. Choose Him now when you can still walk, breathe, and love. Because He's already chosen you.

Chapter 4
FINAL WORDS: THE INVITATION

So, that's my story. That's how a simple trip to the dentist turned into an encounter with the Living God on three separate occasions, shifting my life. Only God would do something like that, right? Because the way I see it, He'll use *anything* to get your attention. Even a gas mask and a thirty-minute oral surgery. And if He did all that for me, you better believe He'll meet you too, wherever you are—however He needs to.

Now, I'm not saying you should go looking for a "near-death experience" to find Him. *Please don't.* But what I am saying is: when He comes for you, let Him in because that's where life really begins. However, let me keep it all the way real for a second. He might, and I mean that's a *huge* might, give you a second chance the way He did for me. But don't count on that. Don't wait until your world starts spinning and the lights start fading to decide you want to know Him. By then, baby, you'll *meet* Him one way or another. So, do yourself a favor:

Get it right the first time.

Choose Jesus not out of fear, but out of love. Because here's the thing: I'd rather have been serving the one true living God and find out I didn't need Him than to have needed Him and realize I didn't *have* Him because I swiped left. You know what I mean. I declined the invitation. And listen, there's no pressure. But also? There's purpose. Every breath you take is a reminder that God still has work for you to do. And I hope my story reminds you that He's not some distant, silent figure sitting on a throne watching from afar.

    He's personal.
    He's real.
    He's in the details — from your business dreams to your
    dentist visits.

So, if you take anything from this first volume, let it be this:

    The meaning of life is love.
    Love God.
    Love people.
    And love yourself enough to walk in obedience to His
    call. Because at the end of the day, everything else fades.
    Titles fade.
    Money fades.

THE ENCOUNTER

Even memories fade.
But love?
That's eternal.

Now that you've heard my story, I want to hear *yours*. For real, this isn't a one-way conversation. You can connect with me and other believers walking this same journey inside "**The Invested Encounter's**" community, where we laugh, we cry, we share, and most importantly, we grow. Because this isn't just a story, it's the beginning of a movement. Sometimes you need a safe space to talk about the wild, unexplainable things God does in your life. And trust me, when you start walking closely with Him, you're going to have encounters too. So... join us.

Rest with me between releases.
Take breaks when you need them.
Apply the wisdom God gives you.
And never stop seeking Him.
So let this journey really begin.
Not with fear.
Not with performance.
But with love pure and simple.

At the end of the day, love isn't what God *does*; it's who He *is*. And once you've met Him for yourself, you'll never be the same. *To be continued...*

Volume 2 - The Encounter of Intimacy

Join "The Encounters." Email **Encounter@communitydts.com** to receive your access code and step-by-step guide to joining.:

- Exclusive devotionals and live sessions
- Faith, business, and family talks
- Early access to upcoming releases and events
- Private prayer groups & accountability teams

Because sis (and bro), you don't have to walk this out alone. We're building a community of believers learning how to truly *follow Christ* one encounter at a time. So, what about you? Are you ready to follow Him, hear His voice, and trust the process no matter what? Have you ever missed God's guidance because you were distracted or trying to follow your own path? The real tea is COMING SOON, but until then, just take a few minutes right now to pray, repent, or even simply welcome God into your life. The following are some prayers I believe will help you.

PRAYER TO BECOME A FOLLOWER OF CHRIST

"God, I'm ready."

Father, I come to You today just as I am, not pretending to be perfect, not hiding what I've done, but bringing You all of me.

I believe that Jesus is Your Son, that He died for my sins, and that He rose again so I could have eternal life. Lord, I open my heart to You right now. Come in and make me new. Teach me how to follow You, to walk in Your ways, and to trust You with my whole life. From this day forward, I give you everything: my past, my pain, my plans, and my future.

I choose You, Jesus. Be my Savior, my Lord, and my best friend. Thank You for saving me and for loving me even when I didn't love myself.

In Jesus' name... *Amen.*

PRAYER FOR FORGIVENESS

Lord, I come before You with an honest heart. I've made mistakes, I've said things, done things, and thought things that don't reflect who You've called me to be. I've tried to fix myself, but I can't do it without You.

So today, I'm asking for Your forgiveness. Wash me clean, Lord. Remove the guilt, the shame, and the weight of my past. Help me forgive myself the way You've forgiven me.

Thank You for Your mercy that never runs out, and for grace that covers every wrong turn I've ever made. I receive Your forgiveness right now, and I choose to walk in freedom, not condemnation. In Jesus' name... Amen.

PRAYER FOR REPENTANCE

Father, I'm turning back to You. I don't just want to say "sorry," I want to *change*. Change the way I think, the way I speak, the way I live.

Create in me a clean heart, O God, and renew a right spirit within me. Show me the areas I need to surrender the habits, the attitudes, the relationships that pull me away from You. Give me the strength to walk in obedience, and the courage to let go of anything that doesn't honor You. I don't want to just know *about* You. I want to live for You. In Jesus' name... Amen.

PRAYER FOR REDEDICATION

Lord, I'm coming home. I know You've never left me, even when I drifted away, You kept calling me back. And today, I'm answering that call. I rededicate my life to You, Jesus. Every part of me, my heart, my mind, my will, all belong to You.

Restore my fire.
Reignite my passion for Your Word.
Renew my joy in Your presence.

Help me to walk boldly in purpose and truth, and surround me with people who push me closer to You, not farther away. Thank You for never giving up on me. From this moment forward, I'm Yours again fully and forever. In Jesus' name... Amen.

* * *

Welcome to a fresh start guided in love, protected in spirit, and provided for by faith! You're off to a great start. Now grab your "33 Days of Developing the Encounter" journal and start your journey today. Why wait? What are you expecting God to do for you today, and then what is he saying?

So, I guess you're still wondering how to identify God's voice from your own. Well… shhh, only the Invested Encounters get this scoop! Lock in. I'll give you a little taste of what's coming in Volume 2: ***The Encounter of Intimacy***, but first…

RANDOM KI THOUGHT

Thank you for spending some time with me; you're pretty awesome yourself! I can hear you thinking, "Yeah, right, you don't even know me." But if you ask my family, they'll tell you that anyone who can handle me for as long as you have is truly remarkable. Haha!

So, I know what you're probably thinking, "Okay, girl, just believe God already." Trust me, I wish it were that easy. One day, I was sitting in my car and I asked God, "Why is it so hard to believe in You sometimes?" And I remember Him showing me something so clearly, almost like a vision. He showed me that even if someone set the building I was sitting in front of on fire and everyone walked out completely untouched, people would still find a way to credit something else. Or, if there was a car accident—the car completely totaled—but the person walked away unharmed, folks would be amazed in the moment. However, a few days later, they'd move on and forget they had even witnessed a miracle.

It was in that moment that I could understand how Peter and the disciples must've felt, questioning things even while walking with the Messiah Himself. Because the Bible says that Jesus told them it's greater for those who believe without seeing than for those who saw Him and believed. And honestly? I'm more like doubting Thomas. Like, "Lord, I gotta see it for myself." Yeah, I hear what everyone's saying, but I still be like, "Let me see though."

Jesus didn't have to appear to Thomas, but He did. He let him put his fingers in the holes in His hands, real flesh, not spirit. Thomas said, "Unless I see the nail marks in His hands and put my finger where the nails were, and put my hand into His side, I will not believe" (John 20:25). And even though I've had my own "Thomas and Jesus" moments in my life, I still find myself questioning sometimes. I know, I know, don't judge me, because I'm sure you do too. It feels like my faith is always being tested. You can probably tell by all the encounters I've had, lol. It doesn't stop here. Turn the page to check out the encounter leading into "Volume 2: The Encounter of Intimacy."

Sneak Peek

VOLUME 2: THE ENCOUNTER OF INTIMACY

Hey, friend!

So, I guess you're still wondering how to identify God's voice from your own. Well… shhh, only the **Invested Encounters** get this scoop! Lock in. I've got something exciting for you… "Volume 2: *The Encounter of Intimacy*" is almost here, and I wanted to give you a little sneak peek. This one's all about hearing God clearly, following His direction, and building a relationship with Him that actually works in real life. Following is a taste of what you'll find inside:

Real Talk: Hearing God vs. Everything Else

Ever wonder if it's God speaking to you or just your own thoughts, or even someone else's agenda? I get it. I've been there. And in Volume 2, I share my own experience with a prophet—someone who revealed things that blew my mind... until some things started to feel off. I learned firsthand that even when someone seems "holy," if it doesn't line up with Scripture or your own peace in God, you need to pause. That's why this book is about *helping you hear God for yourself,* without relying on anyone else to interpret Him for you.

Lessons From My Journey

I was walking in obedience, giving generously, following instructions, but I realized I hadn't prayed through everything personally. I didn't have clarity. And that's when I learned one of the most important lessons:

Never move ahead spiritually without seeking God first

Volume 2 dives into moments like this, distractions, missed signs, and the subtle ways the enemy tries to pull you off course. But it also shows how prayer, Scripture, and discernment can protect you and guide you straight to God's plan.

Write-Along Steps to Hear God Clearly

Inside, I guide you step-by-step to:

- Get under godly leadership (without losing your own connection to God)
- Follow God's vision, not just the work you see around you

- Pray for clarity and confirmation from the Holy Spirit
- Study Scripture daily to align your heart with God. Stay consistent, patient, and focused—even when it's hard.

Plus, I share a simple and powerful *Five-Finger Prayer technique* to pray for yourself, family, friends, your community, and leaders in just a few minutes a day.

Why This Book Matters

If you're ready to experience God personally, grow spiritually, and gain clarity in your faith, this volume is for you. "Volume 2: *The Encounter of Intimacy*" isn't just a book; it's a guide to help you:

- Recognize God's voice clearly
- Stay obedient in real-life situations
- Avoid confusion, deception, and misalignment
- Strengthen your personal walk with God

Coming Soon

I can't wait to share the full journey with you. Pre-order details are coming soon—but for now, consider this your *inside look at the wisdom, guidance, and real-life stories* that will change how you connect with God so that you can hear Him more clearly.

Story Time: My Encounter With a Prophet

Here's the thing—throughout history, people have tried to twist God's original design for their own purposes. And I want you to follow me on this, because this story is going to show you why it's so important to hear from God for yourself.

Okay, so here's what happened. I was introduced to a prophet by a lady I was working with. At first, I was fascinated—this man revealed things that only my family and God knew. I'm talking about stuff that blew my mind.

But here's the thing: over time, things started contradicting each other. At first, everything seemed to line up with God's word, but as time went on, certain things didn't sit right with me, especially after sowing pretty much all that I had. My spirit began to question: *Is this really from God? Or is something else going on?* (Scam likely)

Now, don't get me wrong. The Bible tells us not to disrespect God's anointed or harm prophets. I don't know if this individual was being deceptive or thought he was doing right, but it gave me a feeling of divination. And you know what? I'm only speaking my truth here, what I felt, what I saw, and what I learned, but we'll stop here for now!

- **Reflection Prompt:** Can you recall a time when something seemed spiritual but didn't sit right in your spirit? What did your heart tell you?

- **The Bible warns us to discern the truth:** even when someone speaks in Jesus' name, deception can be entwined with truth.

- **Action Step:** Write down any current guidance you are receiving. Ask God to show you what is truly from Him.

Distortion of God's Original Intent

Here's the truth: when God's original intent gets twisted, failure is almost guaranteed. Misguided agendas, mixed messages, and confusion are the result. And let me tell you, when the source is off, everything that comes from it is unreliable. I followed this man because he spoke in Jesus' name and quoted Scripture. At first, it all seemed right. But then, little things started to feel off. Certain things didn't give me peace. That's why I always say, "Seek God for yourself. Don't rely on what anyone else says, even if it seems holy."

- Misguided intentions lead to actions that may seem righteous but lack divine alignment.
- Lack of authenticity creates doubt and confusion.
- Unforeseen consequences hurt both you and others.
- Inevitable failure occurs when integrity is compromised.

When You Give Everything, But It Feels Off

I was walking in wholehearted obedience, giving tens of thousands of dollars because I thought that's what God wanted me to do. But here's the kicker, I hadn't fully prayed about it myself. I didn't have clarity first. So, if you take anything from this sneak peek, let it be this: *never move ahead spiritually without seeking God first* because even a pure heart can end up following the wrong direction if you're not tuned in. So with that being said, yeah, I'm just going to end it on this note before I get ahead of myself AGAIN!

Learning From My Encounter

- **Reflection Prompt:** Are there areas of your life where you may have followed a plan or advice without fully seeking God first?

- **Action Step:** Before acting on spiritual guidance from others, pause. Pray and ask God directly for confirmation.

- **Final Thoughts:** Signs, Distractions, and Staying the Course

Hearing God, following Him, and staying obedient are not always easy. You will face distractions. You will feel confused. But when you pray, stay in the Word, and seek Him first, clarity comes. And remember: His plan is always better than ours.

See, after traveling far and facing delays, confusion, and distractions, I realized God had been showing me the way all along. He gives signs, but it's up to us to be attentive and obedient. Prayer, Scripture, and a keen spirit will keep you aligned.

"But the Advocate, the Holy Spirit,
whom the Father will send in my name,
will teach you all things and will remind you
of everything I have said to you."

-John 14:26

Afterword

So, what about you? Are you prepared to follow Him, listen to His voice, and trust the journey no matter the circumstances? Have you ever overlooked God's guidance because you were distracted or focused on your own path? I know I have, and I believe God has sent me to help steer you through my mistakes that transformed into miracles.

More tea is *coming soon*, but until then, thank you for your support. I pray this journey has been a blessing for you so far, and of course, *I love you* with the love of Christ.

until next time…

Made in the USA
Coppell, TX
07 January 2026

68174096R10046